MOBA GAMES

BY ASHLEY GISH

Apex is distributed by North Star Editions:
sales@northstareditions.com | 888-417-0195

Produced for Apex by Red Line Editorial.

Photographs ©: iStockphoto, cover; Shutterstock Images, 1, 4–5, 6, 7, 8–9, 10–11, 12–13, 14–15, 16–17, 18, 19, 20–21, 22–23, 24, 25, 26–27, 29

Library of Congress Control Number: 2022920700

ISBN
978-1-63738-573-9 (hardcover)
978-1-63738-627-9 (paperback)
978-1-63738-729-0 (ebook pdf)
978-1-63738-681-1 (hosted ebook)

Printed in the United States of America
Mankato, MN
082023

NOTE TO PARENTS AND EDUCATORS

Apex books are designed to build literacy skills in striving readers. Exciting, high-interest content attracts and holds readers' attention. The text is carefully leveled to allow students to achieve success quickly. Additional features, such as bolded glossary words for difficult terms, help build comprehension.

TABLE OF CONTENTS

CHAPTER 1

THE BATTLE BEGINS

Two teams enter the *League of Legends* battlefield. One champion, Caitlyn, runs to the bottom **lane**.

In *League of Legends*, the battlefield is split into top, middle, and bottom lanes.

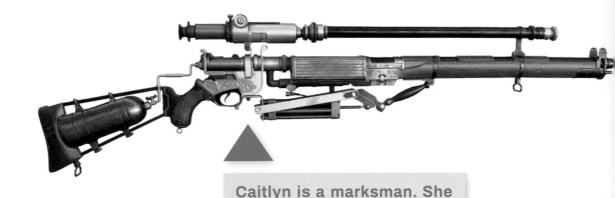

Caitlyn is a marksman. She can shoot faraway enemies with a magic rifle.

Enemy minions appear in the lane ahead. Caitlyn blasts them with her rifle. Then she comes face-to-face with Vi. Vi is a champion from the other team.

Vi wears huge gloves called gauntlets. She uses them to punch and crush enemies. ▶

Vi is ready to fight. But Caitlyn runs away. She tries to find her teammates. They work together to defeat the other team.

MANY CHAMPIONS

In *League of Legends*, players fight as characters called champions. There are more than 140 champions. Each one has different weapons and skills. Each team has minions, too. Computers control these fighters.

Some champions use magic. Others fight with guns or swords.

CHAPTER 2

WHAT MOBA MEANS

MOBA stands for "multiplayer online battle arena." Two teams fight one another in a set area. This area is split into sections called lanes.

Each lane looks like a path. It runs across the arena.

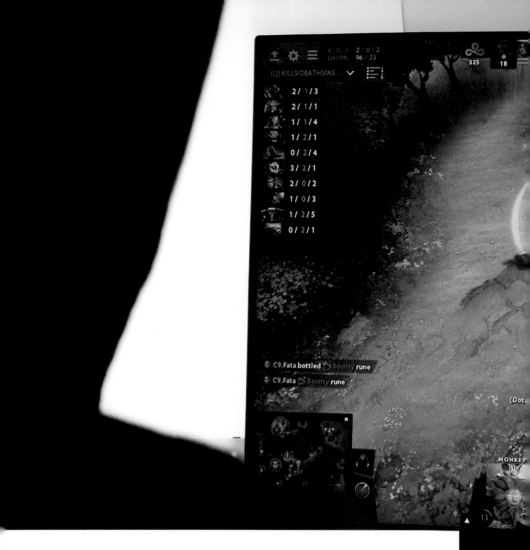

Each team is made up of three to five players. They try to destroy the other team's base. Team bases are at the ends of the lanes.

Some players help defend their team's base. Others focus on attacking.

FAST FACT

Many MOBA games have three lanes. The area between lanes is called the jungle.

Mobile Legends is one of the most popular MOBA games. Players can choose from more than 100 heroes.

Game Loading...

Players work together to attack and defend. Often, each player has a different role. Each focuses on one task or area.

CHOOSING CHARACTERS

A MOBA gamer often fights many times as the same character. With each win, this character gains money or **experience**. That helps the gamer get better weapons or powers.

CHAPTER 3

MOBA HISTORY

StarCraft was released in 1998. This game let players **customize** maps. One player made a map called "Aeon of Strife." It became the first MOBA.

Zerg Larva

25/25

MENU

StarCraft is a video game set in outer space.

Another MOBA was based on *Warcraft III: Reign of Chaos*. A player made a **mod** in 2003. He called it "Defense of the Ancients," or DotA. Fans loved it.

DotA 2 came out in 2013. This updated version was even more popular.

DotA 2 kept many characters from the first DotA game.

REAL-TIME STRATEGY

StarCraft and *Warcraft III* are both **real-time strategy** games. Players build bases and create fighters. Players send their fighters to destroy one another's bases.

Companies began making **original** MOBA games. In 2009, Riot Games made *League of Legends*. By 2012, it was the most popular video game in the world.

In 2021, Riot Games released a version of *League of Legends* that people could play on smartphones.

CHAPTER 4

MOBA IN ESPORTS

Many people play MOBA games in **tournaments**. They compete against other teams. Winners often get prizes.

MOBA tournaments often have rounds. Teams try to win several games in a row.

Tournaments often focus on one game. For example, both *DotA 2* and *League of Legends* have world **championships**. To play in them, teams must win other smaller events.

The International is *DotA 2*'s world championship. It features the best teams from many countries.

Pokémon UNITE can be played on a smartphone or Nintendo Switch.

A NEW MOBA

Pokémon UNITE was released in 2021. Players fight as creatures called Pokémon. They can capture wild Pokémon, too. The first *Pokémon UNITE* world championship took place in 2022.

Gamers who compete at tournaments are called esports players.

Big tournaments can involve thousands of players. Many fans come to see them. Even more people watch online.

FAST FACT

Top MOBA players can earn lots of money. Some colleges offer **scholarships** for esports, too.

COMPREHENSION QUESTIONS

Write your answers on a separate piece of paper.

1. Write a few sentences describing the main ideas of Chapter 4.

2. Do you play any MOBA games? Why or why not?

3. How many lanes are in a typical MOBA game?

    A. two

    B. three

    C. five

4. Which game was "Defense of the Ancients" based on?

    A. *StarCraft*

    B. *Warcraft III*

    C. *League of Legends*

5. What does **role** mean in this book?

Often, each player has a different **role.** *Each focuses on one task or area.*

    A. a job to do

    B. a game to win

    C. a story to tell

6. What does **compete** mean in this book?

They **compete** *against other teams. Winners often get prizes.*

    A. try to win

    B. pay money to

    C. stay away from

Answer key on page 32.

GLOSSARY

championships

Events that decide the best players in a league or sport.

customize

To change something so it fits a certain goal or plan.

experience

Skills or knowledge as a result of doing something.

lane

A pathway from one team's base to another.

mod

A change to how a game looks or is played.

original

New, not based on something else.

real-time strategy

Having players act all at once instead of in turns.

scholarships

Money given to students to help pay for education.

tournaments

Competitions where players try to win several games
or rounds.

TO LEARN MORE

BOOKS

Abdo, Kenny. *League of Legends*. Minneapolis: Abdo Publishing, 2023.

Rathburn, Betsy. *Online Gaming*. Minneapolis: Bellwether Media, 2021.

Schwartz, Heather E. *The History of Gaming*. North Mankato, MN: Capstone Press, 2020.

ONLINE RESOURCES

Visit **www.apexeditions.com** to find links and resources related to this title.

ABOUT THE AUTHOR

Ashley Gish has authored more than 60 juvenile nonfiction books. She earned her degree in creative writing from Minnesota State University, Mankato. Ashley lives in Minnesota with her husband and daughter.

INDEX

ANSWER KEY:
1. Answers will vary; 2. Answers will vary; 3. B; 4. B; 5. A; 6. A